Everyone Has a Story

Everyone Has a Story

Using the Hero's Journey and Narrative Therapy
to Reframe the Struggle of Mental Illness

Andy Matzner, MA, LCSW

Disclaimer

This book is made available with the understanding that the author is not engaged in offering specific medical, psychological, or emotional advice. The information, ideas, and suggestions in this book are not intended to be a substitute for professional care. Each person is unique and this book cannot take those individual differences into account. Any person suffering from a serious mental illness should consult with a clinician before practicing the exercises in this book. The author therefore accepts no liability or responsibility for any results, outcomes, or consequences of the use of content, ideas or concepts expressed or provided in this book.

All rights reserved. No part of this book may be reproduced or transmitted in any form or by any means, electronic or mechanical, including photocopying, recording or by any information storage and retrieval system, without written permission from the author, except for the inclusion of brief quotations in a review.

Copyright © 2015, Andy Matzner

Emancipate yourself from mental slavery, none but ourselves can free our minds!

Marcus Garvey

Epiphany: A sudden insight or intuitive understanding

The purpose of the activities in this book is to foster an environment in which epiphanies may occur.

To be a person is to have a story to tell.

Sam Keen and Anne Valley-Fox

Don't be satisfied with stories, how things have gone with others. Unfold your own myth.

Rumi

We don't know who we are until we hear ourselves speaking the drama of our lives to someone we trust to listen with an open mind and heart.

Sam Keen

Don't forget - no one else sees the world the way you do, so no one else can tell the stories that you have to tell.

Charles de Lint

Our experience quite literally is defined by our assumptions about life…We make stories about the world and to a large degree live out their plots. What our lives are like depends to a great extent on the script we consciously, or more likely, unconsciously, have adopted.

Carol Pearson

While not everyone has had the opportunities I've had, everyone has his or her own version of my story - that moment when you become aware of the thing that will animate and fulfill you, and that period of struggle when you try to find a way to live a life that places your personal passion at the center.

John Legend

When we look at the world through the lens of dollar votes, we see an almost insatiable human demand for stories. Books, movies, and television are multibillion-dollar industries, and their primary business is storytelling. Even music, like poetry, is primarily the art of storytelling set to melody. The fact that we spend so much money on stories – in good times and bad – demonstrates that stories offer something that we really want, not just something we like to say we want. And what most stories offer is the vicarious experience of transformation.

Of course, the tragic part of this analysis is that for most of us, this urge toward transformation remains vicarious, and I believe this is the reason we often feel a bit of a letdown after even the most inspiring stories. Somewhere deep inside, we realize that just as we can't pay someone else to go to the gym, we can't be transformed secondhand, either.

August Turak

Our internalized interpretations drive our daily management systems and create patterns with which we become acculturated and come in time to call our lives.

James Hollis

So, what is the 'real' story of our lives? Are they all real or all unreal, all provisional? There are the stories we tell ourselves, and the stories we tell others. Some of them may even be true. But what are the stories which are storying their way through our daily lives and of which we are mostly if not wholly unaware? What are the stories that represent our rationalizations, our defenses, the stories in which we remain stuck like flies in molasses…

All of us suffer the fallacy of overgeneralization, namely, what was 'true,' or appeared true, remains a defining point of reference, a prompting script for us in ever-new situations. What past wounds to our self-esteem show up today in our deflections from our deepest truths or our overcompensation and grandiosity in reaction to scripts foreign to our souls? What stories did we acquire as children, what marching orders did we receive to serve in the remaining chapters of our history? Were we to be the unseen child, the fixer, the scapegoat, the marginalized? How do those stories persist in the present?

James Hollis

How do we accept...that we are not our history but our unfolding journey?

James Hollis

Table of Contents

Introduction..1

The Hero and the Journey............................11

The Myths We Live, the Stories We Tell..........21

Exploring Your Current Story........................47

Mental Illness / Substance Abuse..................59

Looking Towards the Future.........................65

Appendix: Creating a Manifesto.....................75

Introduction

Picture the following...

An ordinary person experiences something extraordinary...Is then faced with a difficult choice...Decides to set off on a journey into the Great Unknown...Encounters challenges...Discovers a way to overcome them...And finally returns home a changed person, bearing the fruits of their experiences to share with their community.

This narrative, found in myths and legends throughout the world's cultures, was explored by Joseph Campbell in his book *The Hero With a Thousand Faces*. But it does not just apply to larger-than-life characters such as Hercules, Dorothy or Rocky. For when a person struggles with mental illness or addiction, they too face a journey of heroic proportions. Their trials and tribulations, as well as the rewards they experience, closely mirror the stages of the classic "Hero's Journey."

Consider the parallels:

A person's "normal" reality – life as they know it – shifts when they start to experience the symptoms of a mental illness or the effects of a substance abuse problem. This leads to a difficult decision: What to do next.

"Should I seek treatment from a professional or try to handle this on my own?"

"Meds or talk therapy?"

"Maybe I'll just ignore what I am feeling. Perhaps if I try hard enough it will go away."

"I can't believe people are giving me a hard time about my drinking...I haven't changed – they have!"

"I refuse to accept what is happening to me!"

"Do I have this drink? Or not?"

"I need help. Whom do I trust enough to share this with?"

The direction a person takes at this important crossroads determines how their story unfolds. Whether or not a person actively engages in treatment, the fact is that their lives will never be the same. Dealing (or not dealing) with a mental illness or substance abuse problem means that a person's life begins to change as they are forced to grapple with challenges both personal and interpersonal.

The metaphor of a "journey" connects with The Substance Abuse and Mental Health Services Administration's definition of "recovery" as:

"A ***process*** of change through which individuals improve their health and wellness, live self-directed lives, and strive to reach their full potential." (www.samsha.gov/recovery; italics added)

Accordingly, as mental health workers we must ask ourselves how we may best stimulate and then support that "process of change." The answer lies in partnering with our clients in order to help them achieve introspection, hope, self-belief, determination, purpose and meaning in their lives.

At the same time, recovery does not mean ignoring or minimizing psychological symptoms. As Peter Watkins writers,

"[Recovery is the] acceptance and understanding of personal vulnerabilities and the development of strategies to minimize their impact. It is concerned with rebuilding identity, self-esteem and a fulfilling life. It is about recovering and sustaining well-being, sometimes in the context of continuing symptoms."

Therefore, an important goal on the journey to recovery is exploring the meaning(s) that distressing experiences and events have had on a client's life. If those meanings have been negative, it is up to the clinician to assist their client in learning how to reframe those experiences from pathological to positive. This is done by viewing distressing events as existential opportunities for a client to come to understand three things: Who they truly are; where they are going in life; and what is motivating them at their core.

So, why might the "Hero's Journey" be so special? What is there about it that could be healing and empowering for our clients?

I believe that viewing recovery from mental illness or substance abuse as a "Hero's Journey" can shift the perspectives of our clients in several important ways. First, the Hero's Journey" is a **story** with a beginning, middle and end. Taking a narrative view of their own lives of leads our clients to reflect on their past and present situations in a manner that they are most likely not used to doing. But it is that very reflection that creates the opportunity for clients to see the bigger picture of their lives. Looking at one's life as an over-arching story made up of a series of shorter stories provides a unique perspective. It allows a person to make connections between seemingly unconnected events. It creates **order** out of suffering, confusion and randomness. It provides "The Big Picture" of one's life. And if nothing else, humans are meaning-seeking animals; when we are unable to find meaning in our lives, we suffer.

Stepping back and viewing their life as a series of discrete chapters, each with a beginning, middle and end, clients learn how to create an autobiography – and in doing so gain a holistic and coherent way of understanding who they are and why. They can see how their lives naturally fall into specific time periods, each with positive and negative experiences. By examining their pasts – what happened to them and how they responded to what happened – clients slowly become conscious of the values, assumptions, ideals, and ideologies which have influenced the ways in which they think, feel and act. In addition, taking a broader view of their histories also allows clients to more easily locate the patterns, messages and themes that have consistently appeared throughout their lives.

Second, the framework of the Hero's Journey illustrates that nothing, whether good or bad, stays the same forever. Chapters are always unfolding; beginnings, middles and ends are in constant flux. The vital implication is that when a client experiences hardship, it does not necessarily mean the end of the story. Instead, a distressing experience might actually signal the beginning of an adventure by providing an opportunity for growth and self-discovery. Thus, a mental health issue does not have to be an ending! For example, receiving a diagnosis should not mean that now a person will be "stuck" there for the rest of their life. Rather, it can be seen as the beginning of a life-changing path leading to personal development and positive self-growth.

So instead of inhabiting a static label that is frozen in time (e.g. "I am borderline. I am an addict. I have anxiety. I am schizophrenic.") clients learn that life is movement, not stasis, and that the fluidity of life means that each moment is different from the other. Indeed, our story truly doesn't end until our death – which means there is always potential for change. As the Roman philosopher Cicero succinctly put it two thousand years ago, "While there is life, there is hope."

Third, the Hero's Journey illustrates how, far from being the passive recipient of a diagnosis, clients can access their personal power in order to **engage with** the symptoms of their mental health issues and the core issues underlying them. This is significant due to the **stigma** surrounding mental illness in our society. For many people, having a mental illness indicates personal weakness and therefore leads to feelings of shame. Experiencing stereotypes, discrimination, misunderstanding and social exclusion creates embarrassment and a sense of helplessness. In turn, it makes adaptive sense for a person experiencing such things to socially isolate or keep a mental illness diagnosis a secret from others.

The Hero's Journey perspective challenges such stigma, as it allows clients to reframe their mental health issues as the catalysts for a spiritual quest to discover their true selves. Seeing their mental health challenges in this light makes it easier to develop the motivation and strength to stay the course as they move towards healing. Clients learn that there is wisdom to be found in the difficulties associated with mental health issues. After all, it is what challenges us that has the potential to bring forth our heroic qualities. Sister Joan Chittester writes:

I learned that struggle tempers the steel of the soul. It straightens the backbone and purifies the heart. It makes demands on us that change us forever and make us new. It shows us who we are. Then we make choices, maybe for the first time in life, that determine not only what we'll do for the rest of our life, but what kind of person we'll be for the rest of it.

By viewing their lives in the larger context of a story in which they are the author (in terms of how they respond rather than react to what is happening to them), clients learn that setbacks are an inevitable part of the journey to recovery. Significantly, this perspective views obstacles as opportunities for fresh insights and positive change. And so clients discover that they have the capacity to live through distress and can even grow from the experience. So instead of thinking, "I have depression / PTSD / borderline personality disorder / anxiety and that's it, I'm on meds for the rest of my life" or "I'm an alcoholic and I'm broken and this is who I am forever," clients learn to view their "problem" as an opportunity for self-growth.

Therefore, dealing with a mental illness or substance abuse problem becomes a stimulus for both self-reflection as well as deliberate action in service of one's soul. The result is a person learning how to address their suffering in such a way as to develop a deeper, more profound understanding of who they really are and what it means to be human. A person able to discover **meaning** in their pain. Far from remaining passive consumers, clients learn how to become active agents in their lives as they purposefully engage in their process of recovery.

Finally, by recognizing that each person's heroic journey is uniquely theirs, clinicians can recognize and acknowledge clients as the experts of their own lives, and help them learn that there is no "right" or standard way to handle a mental health issue. Rather than experiencing a cookie-cutter, one-size-fits-all approach to their issues, clients come to realize that their journey is a personal process and that there are many possible routes to recovery. There are infinite ways to be heroic, and focusing on the ways a client has demonstrated "heroism" in their life (through their strengths, resources, skills and activities) is truly empowering. This kind of affirmation on the part of a clinician communicates – and sustains – the belief that **all** people have the potential to grow and change in life-enhancing ways.

***

In terms of the gifts that the Hero's Journey bears, perhaps there are none better than the following questions. Each radically shifts the focus from the traditional disease model (in which a "mental illness" is something negative that needs to be "treated" or medicated away) to a perspective that sees mental and emotional distress as an opportunity for personal development and self-growth. A client may be doubtful at the beginning of their journey. But by the end, ideally each of these questions will be answered in the affirmative.

- Can my psychological wounds provide me with a better understanding of who I am and what it means to be alive?

- Can I learn to integrate my past experiences (both positive and negative) into my present identity?
- Can I understand that negative events actually have the power to bring out my heroic qualities?
- Is it possible to see emotional suffering as a gift, rather than a curse?

***

In this book, you will learn how to apply the principles of the Hero's Journey and narrative therapy to your own life as well as to the lives of your clients. Using these perspectives can instill a sense of hope and perseverance. Each one of us has a story to tell; each one of us has a hero or heroine within – the challenge is learning to access and honor those parts of ourselves.

By empowering our clients to understand the journeys that they have taken in their lives, and to gain a broadened perspective regarding their current situation, they will come to view themselves less as victims and more as the heroes of their own stories. Clients will learn how to become aware of when they fall into old myths and, through mindfulness, how to re-frame them. Such awareness allows our clients to free themselves from ways of being in – and reacting to – the world that cause them pain and distress. As they develop the courage to face their stories and then move into the future armed with clarity about their past, healing truly begins.

Therefore, the first step in making any kind of change is increasing one's awareness. The journaling questions and activities in this book will assist your clients in becoming conscious of their own story-telling and myth-making processes. Ideally, they will learn that the course of their lives is not set in stone and that their sense of reality has been – and continues to be – influenced by both internal and external factors. This understanding will provide clients with a sense of control that will allow them to consciously decide for themselves how to interpret past and present experiences – as well as shape their futures.

Our journey together in this book will now move on to an examination of what it means to be a "hero" and the details of "The Hero's Journey." When it comes to the activities I have included in this book, I will be addressing you, the reader, directly. After all, if we are going to offer our clients a service, it is vital that we ourselves have had experience navigating it ourselves. But please do not feel compelled to follow what I have written to the letter; this book is meant to stimulate your interest and curiosity about the Hero's Journey (and narrative therapy, with which it goes hand-in-hand). Please feel free to mix and match the ideas and activities that most resonate with you, and that you feel will most benefit your clients.

The Hero and the Journey

A hero is someone who has given his or her life to something bigger than oneself.

Joseph Campbell

A hero is somebody who voluntarily walks into the unknown.

Tom Hanks

A hero is an ordinary individual who finds the strength to persevere and endure in spite of overwhelming obstacles.

Christopher Reeve

Heroes are people who, in a real way, have confronted and changed their identities through the process of some kind of intense difficulty that they had to undergo. This intense difficulty is sometimes consciously chosen and accepted; at other times, it is just thrust upon a person. ...However impossible the endeavor, they take on the challenge and digest whatever hardships they are called upon to endure. In the process, they find within themselves a sense of strength that allows them to shed who and what they were, thereby becoming a completely different kind of person — a hero.

Swami Chetanananda

What are your thoughts about each of these quotes? Do you agree with them? Why or why not?

What qualities do you think make a hero?

Brainstorm a list of famous heroes, past and present. Why would you consider each one a "hero"?

Whom do you personally know that you would consider a hero? Please explain why.

Describe a time you did something that someone else might consider "heroic."

***

In 1949 Joseph Campbell, an American scholar, published a book called *The Hero with a Thousand Faces*. In it, he summarized dozens of myths and legends that he had collected from around the world, concluding that there is a common pattern that runs through each, which he called "the monomyth."

Comparing different stories, Campbell discovered that regardless of cultural background or time period, the main characters typically experienced an adventure that unfolded in a very specific – and predictable – way. Campbell found that this narrative structure – in which a hero or heroine is summoned to an adventure, faces and overcomes numerous challenges, and then returns home a changed person – represents a metaphorical story pattern that has deeply resonated with humans since time immemorial. He believed that the timeless truths contained in the hero's journey have ensured its survival in the stories we continue to tell ourselves and each other in the present day.

Campbell noticed that "the hero's journey" can be divided into a series of stages. These structural elements may differ depending on the details of the story, but the following broad outline of events is typical.

Part 1: The Ordinary World. Here the future hero is introduced to the audience. Unaware of her potential or what lies ahead, she is simply going about her everyday life without realizing that change is on the way.

Part 2: Call to Adventure. Something happens that disrupts the flow of the hero's normal life. This could be an external event or an internal thought or feeling that forces the hero to think twice about the life she is leading. The "call to adventure" consists of a "push" (either internally or externally generated) and then a choice – to continue with the status quo or to make some sort of change.

Part 3: Refusal of Call/Reluctant Hero. Often when a call is heard, the hero either ignores or refuses it. Reasons for this may include a sense of duty or obligation to their current life, fear, insecurity, a feeling of inadequacy, or not wanting to be inconvenienced. Even when it is painful, confusing or unsatisfying, one's current life is still familiar territory. That makes it difficult to leave it behind for an unknown – and potentially challenging – future.

Part 4: The Threshold. This is the point where the person actually begins their adventure, leaving the known limits of their every-day world. By "crossing the threshold," the hero shows, both to others and themselves, that they are fully committed to the journey. It is also true that occasionally, as with Dorothy in The Wizard of Oz, the hero is forced on their journey and has no choice but to move forward in order to survive.

Part 5: Meeting the mentor. Once the hero shows their commitment to the quest, a guide (either human or animal, and sometimes with magical powers) appears in order to offer guidance.

Part 6: The Challenges. Next, the hero will face a series of challenges on their journey. These tests, tasks, or ordeals often come in a series of three. By engaging with these obstacles (sometimes successfully, sometimes not), the hero begins their personal transformation.

Part 7: Into the abyss. This is the greatest challenge of the journey. The dictionary defines abyss as "a deep or seemingly bottomless chasm." The key is that the abyss only *seems* bottomless, which is why it is the most important test for the hero. As a true crossroads – will they give up in defeat or find the strength to move forward? – struggling with the abyss means that the hero is forced to face their greatest doubts and fears – alone.

Part 8: Transformation and revelation. By successfully meeting the challenge of the abyss, the hero "slays the dragon," thereby achieving the original goal of their journey. In passing through the abyss and then moving to the other side, the hero metaphorically dies and is reborn. By doing so, the hero experiences a transformation – and revelation – that changes how they view life and the world around them. This change in consciousness also allows the hero to fully understand what they are truly capable of, in terms of their personal power.

Part 9: The atonement. During this stage, the hero goes through the process of accepting their newly transformed self. This may also include the development of a new, positive relationship with what had been the hero's greatest challenge. The hero often feels a sense of relief and gratitude that feels refreshing; they have nothing left to prove, either to themselves or others.

It is interesting to note that today we define "atonement" as "a reparation for a wrong or injury." Yet its religious sense of the "reconciliation of God and humanity through Jesus Christ," appears to be closer to the actual etymological roots of the word from *adunare*, meaning "unite" in Latin (**ad**: to, at + **unum**: one). This led to the old English *atonen*, a contraction of "at one"…which means that atonement, in spite of its pronunciation, really does mean "at-one-ment."

Part 10: The return and the gift. The hero's return to everyday life may be one of the most difficult stages of the journey. Now the challenge is how to retain their hard-won wisdom and share what has been learned with their community. Sometimes this can be frustrating, as the hero discovers that their evolution is difficult for other people to accept or understand. But usually the result of completing their journey means that the hero is finally able to experience a sense of deep peace and belonging back in their old world.

***

Please think about a time in your life during which you encountered an obstacle, challenge or struggle – and succeeded in overcoming it. Perhaps you set a goal of losing weight, learning a new language, finding a new job, moving to a new city or developing a new skill. Maybe you experienced a loss and then managed to make peace with what happened.

In writing, please describe what occurred, using the following framework:

- **The Ordinary World:** What was going on in your life **before** you were faced with something "out of the ordinary"?

- **Call to adventure:** What happened that forced you to reconsider how your life had been going? How did the challenge or obstacle arise?

- **Accepting the call:** What allowed you to make the decision to begin moving in a new direction with your life? Why did you decide to move forward and address the challenge instead of ignoring it?

- **Crossing the threshold:** What were some of the first things you did once you committed yourself to facing your challenge?

- **Meeting the mentors:** Who were some people (or animals) you met that helped you? What did they do for you?

- **Facing the ordeal:** What was the toughest thing about overcoming your challenge? How did you successfully handle it?

- **The hero is transformed and receives a reward:** How did you personally change afterward? How did your life change? What did you know after overcoming your challenge that you had not known before?

- **Hero returns home:** What happened next? How did the "new you" impact the other people in your life?

As you look over what you've written, how easy or difficult is it for you to feel pride in what you were able to accomplish? Could your actions be considered "heroic"? Why or why not?

***

Think about your current life. Are you presently in the midst of a hero's journey? Are you at a cross-roads or facing a challenge? Are you being "called"? If so, how? Are you in the abyss? Is there an achievement you need to honor and celebrate? Please write some notes to yourself about which stage of the journey you are presently on; what will likely happen if you remain stuck at that stage; and what needs to happen for you to move on to the next stage.

Activity: View a film and analyze it in terms of the Hero's Journey framework. As you're watching, see if you can notice when and how the protagonist goes through its various stages. Afterwards, the following questions will help you reflect on what you've just seen.

- How would you summarize the film, using just three sentences?
- Which character was "the hero"?
- What made them heroic?
- What were the strengths of that character?
- What were their weaknesses?
- Was there a point during the film in which the hero became stuck or didn't know what to do next? How did they get un-stuck?
- How did that character transform over the course of the film? What lessons did they learn?
- Which scene in the film made the deepest impression on you? Why?
- What was the greatest challenge that the hero faced? How did they overcome it? Who helped?
- What loss or losses did the hero experience in the film? How did they initially respond to the loss? Did they return to the loss and respond differently to it later in the film?
- Were other characters in the film impacted or influenced by the hero? If so, how?
- How does the film relate to your own life?

Here are some recommended films:

- The Karate Kid
- Top Gun
- Field of Dreams
- The Lego Movie
- Finding Nemo
- The Matrix
- The Crash Reel
- Groundhog Day
- The Devil Wears Prada
- Rocky
- Star Wars
- Castaway
- Silence of the Lambs
- The Lord of the Rings
- Toy Story
- The Princess Bride
- Dead Poets Society
- Apollo 13
- The Lion King
- Crouching Tiger, Hidden Dragon
- The Wizard of Oz
- The Goonies
- The Chronicles of Narnia
- Legally Blond
- Dances with Wolves
- Big Hero 6
- O Brother, Where Art Thou?
- Contact
- Labyrinth

The Myths We Live, The Stories We Tell

I asked myself, 'What is the myth you are living?' and found that I did not know. So...I took it upon myself to get to know 'my' myth, and regarded this as the task of tasks...I simply had to know what unconscious or preconscious myth was forming me.

Carl Jung

...we were all raised by an intimate group that had traditions, values, rites of passage, ceremonies and legends. When we forget our stories, leave our heroes unsung, and ignore the rites that mark our passage from one stage of life into another, we feel nameless and empty.

Sam Keen and Anne Valley-Fox

Because the Hero's Journey is narrative-based (i.e., a story), in this chapter I would like to spend a bit of time focusing on the importance of stories in the process of recovery. After all, as babies we are born into families already saturated with their own narratives, which in turn influence the stories we then tell ourselves (whether consciously or unconsciously) about the world and our place in it. As clinicians, we must assist our clients in becoming aware of their stories, and whether those stories are empowering or disempowering. Doing so will make all the difference in terms of them successfully utilizing the Hero's Journey framework.

Starting as children, the way we make sense of things and view our environment is influenced by a wide variety of factors: parents, extended family, peers, teachers, religion, film, music, television…Thus, the meanings we attach to experiences are colored by the messages we hear, see and feel as we grow up. These messages – the stories (or narratives) we learn about ourselves and the world around us – create the filters through which we interpret life. Carol Pearson writes,

Our experience quite literally is defined by our assumptions about life…We make stories about the world and to a large degree live out their plots. What our lives are like depends to a great extent on the script we consciously, or more likely, unconsciously, have adopted.

Thinking about stories in a therapeutic manner is the foundation of **narrative therapy**, which itself is based on **social constructionism**, a theory that proposes the following four principles:

1. Realities are socially constructed
2. Realities are created through language
3. Realities are organized and maintained through narrative
4. There are no essential truths

Accordingly, the meaning(s) of our lives are based on the stories we tell ourselves about who we are, where we've come from, and what the future holds. And every family has its own stories, its own traditions, its own mythologies about its members and their pasts and what each person in it is capable of...Every family has its own answers to life's Big Questions: Why are we here? What are our duties? Why do bad things happen to good people? What are we supposed to do with our lives? What are we capable of achieving in our lives? What happens after we die? Who are the good guys and who are the bad guys?

Thus, each family has its own cosmology which neatly explains the world and each person's place within it. To ensure that I am being clear, let me give some examples of what I mean by "stories" or "narratives" in this context:

- Growing up, Jimmy discovered that his father hated his job. And because he hated his job, he would come home in a foul mood and start drinking. When Jimmy's father got drunk he would become violent with whomever was around. So Jimmy learned to become invisible. He even learned how to "stop breathing" [his words] so as not to be noticed. The dominant story in Jimmy's life was that safety lay in becoming totally unobtrusive, because attracting attention led to danger.

- Jane's older sister Tammy always got good grades. Their parents liked to compare the siblings and were constantly judging Jane for not being as smart as Tammy. In fact, the parents would often question Jane's intellectual ability out loud in front of her. Jane quickly learned that her story was: I'm the dumb one of the family. It certainly won't be possible for me to academically go far in life. Why even bother?

- Leonard's mother was very tight with her money. She told her son stories about her own parents' experiences during the Great Depression and how she had always had a fear of losing everything and becoming homeless. The only way to guard against such a thing happened was to save as much as possible and not to spend "frivolously." The fear-based lesson for Leonard was that money is to be saved and not spent; risk is dangerous and must always be sacrificed for financial security.

- It seemed like people were always leaving Robert's life. First his father, who abandoned his family soon after Robert's birth. Then, because his mother is a traveling nurse, it's his friends. With a new school every year, Robert becomes intimately acquainted with loss. And then, when he is sixteen, his mother passes away from cancer. Robert tells himself a story of steady betrayal, believing that it is dangerous to get close to people, since they always end up leaving.

- Linda's parents spend a great deal of their time volunteering. A lot of their money also goes to various charities. Growing up, Linda learns that helping others is always the "right thing to do," even if it is inconvenient or financially difficult, because it serves the will of God.

- Food, glorious food! Laura's parents showed both their love and concern with food. When Laura had something to celebrate, her mother baked a cake. When she was upset, her mother made cookies. And for good reason. Laura's mother repeatedly told her how, growing up, her own mother had refused to allow sweets in the house. How unfair! Things would certainly be different now that she were a mother of her own. As for Laura's father, it was hard not to notice that when he was stressed he would turn to food, noisily going through the cupboards looking for things to eat. The story for Laura? That food and eating were not necessarily related to simply being hungry.

- When he was ten, Ben's mother Nancy became unable to work due to severe fibromyalgia. Because his father then got depressed and refused to care his wife, her care fell to Ben. For the next thirteen years Nancy depended on Ben to meet her medical and emotional needs. After Nancy passed away, Ben decided to become a nurse. "It's natural," he thought. "After all, that's what I do. I help people."

- Jacob was a naturally thin child. But his father felt he was too skinny. "You need to put some meat on those bones!" He told Jacob, over and over, as he grew into a young man. "Nobody likes a guy who doesn't look strong." Taking those words to heart, Jacob started going to the gym and lifting weights in his late teens. And he became heavier, more muscular. He continued working out for the next thirty years. Even as he entered his fifties he found it difficult to stop make making regular visits to the gym. "After all," he reasoned, "If I stop going my muscles will shrink, and I'll be skinny again…" And with that he remembered what his father used to say, and shuddered. Not going to happen.

- Mary, in her mid-twenties, was experiencing sleepless nights, alternating with periods of depression. Exhausted (physically and emotionally), she went to a psychiatrist. His message was simple but stern: "You have bipolar II disorder. This is a mental illness that a person doesn't recover from. All you can do is learn how to manage it, with medication." Mary was upset to hear this news but accepted it. After, the psychiatrist had a medical degree, and, as her father used to tell her, "The doctor always knows best."

- Growing up, Barbara watched her father treat her mother very poorly. Overbearing and critical, he was always putting her down and belittling her. Yet her mother suffered in silence for forty years, until Barbara's father passed away from an illness. Barbara had no way of knowing how her mother had managed to stand the situation she found herself in; they never talked about it. But what Barbara *did* learn was that you don't leave a marriage. And so when she found herself with an emotionally abusive husband and her friends begged her to leave him, the refrain she heard looping in her head was: "Regardless of how your spouse treats you, finding someone new isn't an option. It just *isn't*."

***

But how aware are we of the messages and beliefs that guide our lives? Are we conscious of the stories in which we are enmeshed? Do we understand the true origins of the beliefs, influences, and patterns that have made up the fabric of our lives? Are our stories empowering or victimizing? Is it true that the story I have been living, the beliefs I have about myself and the world, encourages me to be the best version of myself?

Or, on the other hand, could it be possible that the messages I internalized while growing up are actually preventing me from exploring or fulfilling my potential in the present time? What if I have become frozen into ways of being that originally helped me cope with events in the past, but which I am still using in the present, long after they are necessary? Could it be that a story that once guided my life, one which perhaps even helped me survive my upbringing, is now draining my life force and slowly (or rapidly) killing me?

The real damage arises from self-deception. Well-intentioned people like you and me are often driven by unconscious fears and hidden agendas – secret agendas so well hidden that they are hidden even from ourselves.

August Turak

Therefore, it becomes imperative to reflect on our past. Doing so gives us access to the bigger picture of where we have been and where we are going. This broadened perspective also allows us to see where we are stuck, where we have blocked our life's flow, and how we can restore movement and meaning. Understanding the patterns of our journey allows us see the greater story that is unfolding in our lives – the connections between events – and to relate current difficulties with that expanded perspective.

And so this is the paradoxical nature of change: In order to move forward, we must first go back and review. After all, as clinicians we cannot force our clients to change. We can only foster an environment in which self-growth flowers naturally, in its own time. One way to do this is to help our clients understand, through self-reflection, the meanings they have given to their lives (as well as the meanings that *others* have given their lives).

But not only that. We also must assist clients in understanding that the particular perspectives they have assigned to past events are not set in stone. It is their *interpretation* that leads them to play either the victim's role or, instead, a role in which they feel empowered. And so it becomes imperative to provide a learning environment in which our clients may discover that *how* they view a past event is mutable; depending on how they focus their attention, they can either highlight their inadequacies or instead acknowledge their strengths.

Unfortunately, the dominant stories of our clients are usually problem-oriented, full of dysfunctional messages. These particular narratives obscure their hopes, dreams, skills, and achievements. Consciously or unconsciously, these stories are oppressive because they negatively influence the beliefs a person has about what is possible for them in life.

This is why it is so important for the clinician to help their client change problem stories into solution stories. By first recognizing and then working to transform a dominant negative storyline, the clinician can help a client focus on events in their life that challenge a problem-saturated narrative. This is done by asking the client to explore their past in order to look for stories and beliefs that they had previously ignored. This is because we usually have filtered out experiences that do not match our dominant story-line. Therefore, it is the goal of the clinician during this stage of treatment to assist the client in recognizing story-lines that have been subordinate to their main narrative; story-lines that actually bring satisfaction and self-worth rather than distress. We want our clients to take a fresh look at themselves and to find significance in experiences and events in their lives that they have neglected or discounted.

This is where the idea that "What we focus on, grows" becomes especially important. Narrative therapy suggests that we create a negative reality by focusing our attention and perceptions on story-lines which support our self-created negative reality. The desire to avoid cognitive dissonance creates a vicious cycle – a closed loop – in which story-lines which are contrary to the dominant negative are not perceived (though they are available) or are brushed aside. That is, if we have internalized a negative story about our life we instinctively will search for negatives to support the 'Truth' of that dominant narrative. The result is that we unintentionally pass over many of the positive experiences in our lives that are contrary to what we believe to true. Simply put, our beliefs influence our perceptions of reality. We see the world (and ourselves) the way we have been taught to.

As we assist our clients in exploring storylines that are different from or contrary to their dominant narrative, they learn how to allow these alternate beliefs into their lives. The clinician helps this "re-writing" by validating this new perspective for the client.

This is why locating stories within the framework of the Hero's Journey can be helpful, since its structure makes it easier to reframe events in a more empowering way. If, for example, a person's story is that they are always the victim, the clinician's goal is to assist the client in carefully examining their history for times in which they were *not* the victim. It is those storylines that the clinician encourages the client to recognize and honor as their new focus.

Indeed, as clinicians we want our clients to understand that they do not have to remain passive spectators of their own lives, but rather that they have the power to take a more active role, both in how they view their past, as well as in the choices they are faced with in their current lives. An important goal is for clients to discover how to engage with their present-day challenges in a way that is action-oriented and life-affirming. Instead of avoiding problems or wishing they didn't exist, they can do one of two things:

1. Focus on what they are able to change.
2. Find some way to make peace with what is beyond their control.

It is this attitude that will empower our clients to persist in moving forward as they change their lives for the better – when in the past it would have been all too easy to simply give up. As the well-known prayer (which should be a cornerstone of any recovery journey) goes:

God grant me the serenity to accept the things I cannot change, the courage to change the things I can, and the wisdom to know the difference.

The point is that when we attribute our success or our failure to forces outside of our control – when we believe that we are passive actors in a role chosen by someone else for us – we give up our personal power to affect what happens in our own lives.

This is why it is so important to explore the past, and examine who and what influenced us to become the person we are today. Certainly, this process can be painful. However, it is vital. This is because we need to be clear about which messages, beliefs, and stories have served us and which have caused us suffering. If we stay stuck in old habits of coping or remain in roles long outdated, we delay embarking on the journey that will allow us to fulfill our potential in life and become the best version of ourselves.

For example, we currently might be using defenses we created in the past to protect ourselves from pain – such as food, alcohol, work, television, or passivity – that are now creating more harm than good. Therefore, before we can begin our journey into the world, we must first journey into ourselves to find and then remove defenses that are blocking our growth.

This is also the paradox of the heroic journey. The first stage of the journey is often not a going forward, but a going back, deconstructing the protective masks and illusions we built in a former life. Then, with the delusions stripped away and our feet firmly planted in the reality of our present, we can gradually begin to move forward again, embracing our potentials and our futures because we are no longer encumbered by the baggage of our past.

Reg Harris

In examining the people, places and things that have influenced our story, we often will discover the origins – and nature – of the baggage that has been preventing us from being authentic and feeling truly alive. It is only by closely exploring and deconstructing our past life that we can understand how and why it was constructed in the manner it was. As we discover who we really are and who we need to be, the ground becomes fertile for developing the courage to begin to move forward on a new journey unconstrained by ideas and habits rooted in the past.

***

In the context of recovery it is especially important for the clinician to assist their client in locating, examining, and then narrating (either in writing, artwork or spoken word) their experiences with **mental illness or addiction**. The clinician will need to explore what stories clients are telling themselves – and have been told about these issues.

As mentioned above, mental illness is surrounded by stigma. Clients often have had distressing experiences because of the ways in which people have responded to them and their struggles. Some of the worst offenders can be family members and health care providers, two groups that are supposed to support clients. Instead, they often end up re-traumatizing our clients by expressing disapproval or judgment. This sense of invalidation can cut deeply, as it fosters a sense that there is something inherently wrong with the client. Narrative therapy counteracts that belief by postulating that a problem is **external** to the person. That is, the problem is not the person; the person is not the same as their "illness."

Consider the following statements:

"I am depressed."

"I am a borderline."

"I am an addict."

"I am anorexic."

"I am a schizophrenic."

"I am an alcoholic."

"I am sick."

When you label yourself (or are labeled by others) as literally being the problem it becomes extraordinarily difficult to encourage change. After all, grammatically "I am" equals ownership. When you say "I am," it is as true and potentially immutable as saying one's name: "I am Andy Matzner." Labeling therefore can lead to over-identification, for better or worse.

In order to address this issue, narrative therapists have asked whether there could be any other way in which clients could characterize their symptoms. Michael White, an Australian family therapist who is a pioneer of narrative therapy, answered this question by developing what he called the **externalization technique**. This is a linguistic strategy in which the clinician approaches a client's problem as if it were separate and distinct from the client. By externalizing the problem, you can give it a name and have a conversation with it. In doing so, a client learns that they are able to dramatically change their relationship with it.

One way to externalize a mental health diagnosis is to turn adjectives into nouns and add a *preposition* to the characteristic or behavior. For example, instead of saying "I am depressed," a client might say "I am struggling with depression." Or replace "I am anorexic," with "I am living with anorexia."

At the same time, "I **have** x" is also problematic, even though in this sentence the "x" is a noun rather than an adjective. For example, a person might say "I have bipolar" or "I have schizophrenia." But what does that even mean? Grammatically, this vague type of sentence exists outside of time. Is it like having a cold that goes away eventually? Or is it like having brown hair, which I have forever (at least until it turns grey)? I believe it is far more clarifying (and empowering) instead to state, "I have a *relationship* with x" or "X is currently a part of my life."

Through externalization, the client is able to see that the problem can be separated from their identity or sense of self (ego) and therefore can be removed or changed. After all, if you believe that a mental health issue is *not* a permanent aspect of your personality, then it becomes significantly easier to initiate the change process. It can be very liberating for a client to see that they are distinct from, and therefore have a degree of control over, the "problem". This distance can allow a client to explore the various choices they have, in terms of how they might interact with their mental health issue.

In particular, narrative therapists are interested in initiating dialogues that they and/or the client can have *with* the mental health issues. In doing so, the clinician can examine – and hear firsthand – how the problem has influenced the client's life. How has the issue been disruptive? How has it caused pain? How has it narrowed their ability to make choices? What benefits does it provide?

At the same time, the clinician and client can explore those times during the client's life when the issue had faded into the background and not been so dominating. The goal is to find and then focus on instances that highlight the strength a client possessed when they successfully were able to manage their issue. These points in time become trailheads for new, empowering narratives for the client.

Below are some examples using the externalization technique with various mental health issues. Notice how the clinician personifies the problem so that the client can actively engage and dialogue with it.

- Instead of "I am depressed," the client could be encouraged to say, "I am currently living with Depression." The therapist could then ask questions such as, "Do you remember when you first met Depression? What was going on in your life at that time?" "What is it like having Depression as a roommate?" "Have you ever successfully resisted Depression? How so?" and "What needs to happen for Depression to move out?"

- "I am paranoid." In this case a clinician might suggest that the client reframe their experience as "being stalked by Paranoia," and ask: "How has Paranoia been cramping your style?" "What sorts of things has Paranoia been saying to you?" "How does it feel having Paranoia in your life?" "Does Paranoia ever give you a break?"

"Have you ever successfully challenged Paranoia? How did you do it?" "Is there something you'd like to tell Paranoia?"

- "I am an alcoholic." To shift a client's perspective, a clinician could ask, "What was the reason that Alcohol decided to come into your life?" "How is Alcohol your friend?" "Does Alcohol ever kick your ass?" "Does Alcohol ever get boring?" "What has Alcohol taught you?"

- "I am anorexic." A clinician might wonder, "Why do you think Anorexia decided to take up residence in your life?" "What would Anorexia like you to believe?" "How do you feel when you are hanging out with Anorexia?" "What are the advantages of having Anorexia in your life?" "Do you feel that Anorexia has overstayed its welcome?" "What could you do to make it easier for Anorexia to decide to pack up and leave?"

The externalization technique can also be used with personality traits. For example, a client might talk about "being a perfectionist." The clinician could reframe this characteristic by asking, "So, tell me – how does Perfectionism keep you busy?" "What does Perfectionism do to distract you?" "What arguments does Perfectionism use to convince you that it is right about things?" "How is your relationship with Perfectionism working for you? How satisfying is it?"

Narrative therapists will often go a step further in the externalization process and ask their client to personify the problem by actually giving it a name. For example:

I am bipolar → I have bipolar → I experience periods of mania and severe depression → I have a relationship with 'Animal' [from the Muppets] and 'Eeyeor" [from Winnie the Pooh]

So how does this aspect of narrative therapy connect with the Hero's Journey? Well, consider the idea that according to Jungian psychology, mental health and substance abuse issues are messengers from our subconscious. Thus, far from being the random effects of a brain chemical imbalance, "mental illness" has an important purpose: To force a person to pay attention to something they are ignoring in their life. So the question becomes, How willing are we to listen to our mental illness? To sit with it instead of ignoring it or numbing ourselves to it through medication? *Are we willing to understand a mental health issue as a call to action, a call to the Hero's Journey?*

Therefore, perhaps the ultimate externalization questions a client can ask their mental health issue or addiction are:

What message do you have for me? What choice are you asking me to make? What are you asking me to *do*?

***

As you can see, stories are important. But **how we tell them** – both to ourselves and to others – is equally important. For narrative therapists, true healing is found in the **act** of telling one's story. It is in the process of reviewing, organizing, and editing one's history that a broader perspective is achieved. And perspective is power, because while we can't always control our situations in life, we can often control our perspective (that is, the meaning we give to a situation).

Think about how dominant stories often are frozen in time in our psyches. That teacher who used to belittle us in front of class every week created a timeless narrative, existing without beginning or end, even though it originally was a series of discrete events. That is why the act of storytelling is so important; reviewing the nooks and crannies of our lives helps us understand that in reality our stories are constantly changing and evolving. That seemingly catastrophic and insurmountable event that swallowed up our being in one moment becomes, in time, just one chapter of the many that end up being written over the course of our lives.

And so, as clinicians, we can assist our clients in meeting that primal human need of reframing experiences with reflection and retelling. Jean Houston writes:

Story is living and dynamic. Stories exist to be exchanged. They are the currency of human growth. Stories conjugate. Alone you are stuck. In the exchange, both you and the story change. Stories need to be told and retold, heard and reheard to reveal their meaning.

Fitting one's life into a narrative structure in order to tell it as a story has a number of advantages. First, it turns chaos into order. Thinking systematically about the past and organizing it chronologically helps us to see our lives in ways we most likely haven't considered before. A careful examination of our history makes it easier to see patterns and the consequences of choices.

Over the last few days, I have been able to see my life as from a great altitude, as a sort of landscape, and with a deepening sense of the connection of all its parts. This does not mean I am finished with life.

Oliver Sacks

Second, as we consider the past, we discover what really made an impact on us and what didn't. We tune into the memories that have never left, the decisions that continue to haunt us or the accomplishments that still fill us with pride. Deciding what to put into our story and what to leave out provides us with important psychological information. Third, a life review makes it easier to remember all of the blessings we have received in our lives. Negative experiences tend to stick in our memories. But what about all those things that have gone right and worked out?

This is why the concept of "story-telling" is an integral part of recovery: In order to give meaning to our journeys we first must reflect on them. But then we must tell them and retell them, both to ourselves and to others. Reflecting on and telling our stories allow us to build a bridge from where we once were to where we currently are. In deciding *how* to tell our stories, we are forced to create meaning, and make narrative decisions about direction, flow and purpose. It also turns our attention to future: Where does my story now lead? Are there chapters that need ending? Or beginning?

To sum up, the goal of narrative therapy is to assist clients in re-authoring their own stories and overcome the dominant narratives that have negatively impacted their interpretations of their experiences in life. The power of the Hero's Journey is found in its demonstration that negative events have the potential to bring forth previously unrecognized heroic qualities.

Consider the implications for being diagnosed with a mental illness. For some people, the diagnosis itself is frightening because of what they have been taught it means: That they are abnormal; inadequate; defective; cursed; doomed; broken...

So...

- What if a clinician could assist this client in seeing that what they "know to be True" about mental illness is actually based on somebody else's idea of the world? That they were *taught* those values?

- What if a clinician could help this client discover and strengthen the overlooked experiences in their lives that challenged their dominant story-line?

- What if a clinician encouraged the client to squarely face their mental health issue and ask two powerful questions:
    o What can I learn from this?
    o Is there anything else this could mean?

- What if this client could learn the skills to **re-tell** their story (to both themselves as well as to others) as one of resilience, strength, survival…and Recovery?

These are the gifts of narrative therapy and the Hero's Journey: As therapeutic perspectives, they ask us to imagine the infinite potentials contained in the "What if's….?"

Questioning is a basic tool for rebellion. It breaks open the stagnant hardened shells of the present, revealing ambiguity and opening up fresh options to be explored…Questioning can change your entire life. It can uncover hidden power and stifled dreams inside of you…things you may have denied for many years.

Fran Peavey

Exploring Your Current Story

Timeline: Divide your life into five year periods, with the first section from birth until five years of age, moving up through your current age. What do you remember being the most significant events that occurred during each of these periods of time? You can create a graph or just write out your timeline in narrative form. Use the following topics as a guide to jog your memory.

- Physical health
- Mental/emotional health
- Relationships
- School / Education
- Spiritual/religious experiences
- Service to others
- Hobbies
- Travel
- Family (caregivers/partners/children)
- Career/Work
- Physical locations (where you have lived)
- Losses

- Substance use/abuse
- Major life changes
- Major life decisions
- Obstacles/set-backs
- achievements

Look for patterns in your timeline. When are periods of freedom and positivity, anxiety and sadness? What else was happening in your life during those times? Are there correlations between certain types of events and your physical/emotional health? Were there periods when your mood or attitude changed? What led to those changes? What happened following those changes? What types of events felt most significant to you? What are the themes of different periods of your life?

***

What are you most proud of, as you think back over the course of your life? What are you most disappointed about? What makes you most sad? Which memories fill you with happiness and joy?

***

Imagine that you were going to write your autobiography; how would you outline it? What would you include? What specific stages does your life naturally seem to fall into? What ages were 'crisis' periods for you? Chapter titles? Subsections? The title of your book?

Now I would like you to actually write your autobiography in the first person ("I"). See if you can keep it to 3 or 4 pages. Once you have finished, I would like you to write it again, but this time using the third person ("she/he"). Read over the story you wrote using the third person. What kind of impression does it make on you? What words would you use to characterize the central character of your story (i.e., yourself)?

Going Deeper

Based on the work you've been doing thinking about your past, who or what would you say has had significant influence on your thoughts, feelings and behaviors over your life? How so?

How have the following had an impact your life, in terms of decisions you made or did not make? In terms of limiting you or empowering you? Go through each one and make some written notes to yourself.

- Parents/caregivers
- Geographical location
- Education
- Religion
- Health (physical/mental)
- Your gender
- Sexuality
- Money
- The media
- Fear

Is there anything or anyone else that has had an influence over how you have lived your life?

***

Values are personal beliefs about what is good and bad, or right and wrong. They are also ideas about what is important to us in life. We typically want more of what we value in our lives and less of what we do not. Accordingly, our values point us in particular directions and steer us away from others. Some of the values we hold are situational, and apply to specific times, contexts, or people. Other values are much more core to who we are and transcend any specific situation. They guide us across all the domains of our lives. These core values determine the people and opportunities we seek out, and the ones we avoid. They shape the goals we set in life, and then motivate us to move toward those goals. Ultimately, they are the standards we use to evaluate our own actions and the actions of others.

<u>**Examples of values:**</u>

Balance; community; family; adventure; safety; affluence; calmness; friendship; discipline; work; honesty; faith; solitude; charity; learning; relaxation; health; thrift; playfulness; athleticism; fun; fame; spirituality; money; travel; nature; comfort; freedom; honor; teamwork; independence; ambition; self-growth; generosity; dependability; flexibility; loyalty; optimism; self-discipline; perfectionism…

Please make a list under the following heading:

These values have been important to me in how I have lived my life:

For each value that you have written, please ask the following: What does this value mean to me? What does this value give me? Why is it important to me? How does it make me feel? Does it empower me or limit me/cause me pain?

***

Core beliefs: These are what we know to be true, both about ourselves and the world around us. It is necessary to realize, however, that we *learn* these truths as we grow up – we are not born with them. Therefore, a very important question to ask yourself is:

Where did my basic assumptions and ideas about myself and the world around me originate?

Often you received these assumptions and ideas from the same people and places that provided you with your original value system:

- Societal norms
- Family
- The media
- Community (peers; friends; religious institutions; teachers)
- Feedback from our own experiences

So consider this: What you consider "reality" might simply be a collection of ideas, perceptions, assumptions, expectations, and opinions that you have come to accept about yourself and the world around you.

Remember, your basic assumptions frame the world you live in and provide the meaning you find in it. But most people are not conscious of their assumptions. This misperception may prevent you from seeing things as they really are. That is, instead of spontaneously *responding* to something in an appropriate manner, you might automatically *react* to it the way you always have. In that sense, your beliefs are triggers, and as such do not allow you to engage with reality on a moment-by-moment basis, since you are trapped in the past.

Below are some examples of negative core beliefs. Notice if any sound familiar to you.

- The world is a dangerous place.
- People can't be trusted.
- Asking for help makes a person appear weak.
- Women shouldn't work.
- Men aren't dependable.
- Life isn't fair.
- I am a bad person.
- I will never fit in.
- I am incapable of being independent.
- I am weak.
- I need other people to validate me.
- I should be able to do whatever I want.
- It's always my fault.

- It's never my fault.
- My needs don't matter.
- People always leave.
- I am unlovable.
- If something isn't *perfect* then it's no good.
- I have no self-control.

Here are some examples of positive beliefs:

- I deserve to be loved.
- I am a worthwhile human being.
- It is OK to ask for help.
- I am unique.
- I have faith in myself.
- I can trust my body.
- It is OK to make mistakes.
- It is OK to be nice to myself.
- I am open to new experiences.
- I am stronger than I realize.
- I won't let perfect get in the way of good enough.
- It is OK to take risks.
- I don't have to be perfect.
- I am strong enough to love another person.
- It is OK for me to receive love and support.
- It is important for me to show my emotions.
- I am willing to make mistakes as long as I learn from them.
- I don't need approval from other people.

The following questions will help you get a sense of what your own belief system consists of:

What three adjectives would you use to describe your father?

What three adjectives would you use to describe your mother?

What are at least three things you learned from your father?

What are at least three things you learned from your mother?

Are there any stories that your mother or father told you that still stick in your memory? What are they? What point was your parent trying to make by telling the story?

Are there any specific conversations or sentences spoken by either your father or mother that you can still remember? What are they? What were the emotions surrounding them?

Based on what you have experienced in your life, what lessons have you learned?

What do you believe to be true about yourself and the world around you?

***

Do you feel that you developed any coping mechanisms as a child to help you feel safe or to deal with stress? Do those coping mechanisms still have an impact on your life? Do they still work? Do they have any negative side effects?

How do you currently cope with stress?

What impact do you feel your childhood experiences have had on your adult life?

How has fear impacted your life and the decisions you have made (or not made)?

Do you have a special skill or talent that comes naturally to you? What is it? How does it make you feel when you're doing it?

Do you have a special skill or talent that you learned on your own or from another person? Not something that you were born with, but instead developed through hard work because you were personally interested in it? How does it make you feel when you're engaged in it?

Looking back over your life, what are (at least) five things or accomplishments you are proud of? What are (at least) five things that you regret?

***

What adjectives would you use to describe your life? If you had to pick a single word to describe your life, which would it be?

A "theme" is an idea or point that is central to a story. What is the theme or themes that sum up your life as a whole?

Return to the chapters of your autobiography. What is the overall theme for each chapter?

What patterns do you notice have played out throughout your life?

Are there specific beliefs that have influenced your life in major ways? Where do you think they came from?

Have you ever felt that you may have been living someone else's story? If so, whose? A parent's? A family's? Society's?

So what is the over-arching story you've been telling to yourself about yourself? How would you summarize your story, as if it were the plot of a movie, in a single sentence?

"This is the story of a ---- who ----"

***

Based upon all of the self-exploration you've been doing, please fill in the following:

- Looking back on my life, I now understand ----
- I will never understand ---
- When I was a child, I didn't realize that ---
- It would take me years to ----
- It would take me years to know that ---
- Everywhere I've gone, I've always carried ---

Pretend you are an outside observer who has read about your life. "This is a person who ----."

***

Finally, I would like you to narrate, in writing, five short stories:

1. What was a setback or obstacle in your life that you eventually overcame? How did you do it? What did you learn from your experience? Begin your story at its lowest point. Then describe what happened from there.

2. Can you remember a moment that changed your life in a positive way? Some awakening or epiphany that shifted everything for you? Was it reading a particular book or article? Watching a film? Meeting a person? Start your story with that profound moment. What happened? How were you transformed?

3. Think of a lesson you have learned in your life. Describe what happened that allowed (or forced) you to learn it. How did learning that lesson impact the rest of your life from that point forward?

4. I would like you to think about a time in your life when you did something that had a positive impact, either on yourself or others. Perhaps you set some important boundaries. Spoke the truth when it needed to be spoken. Took extraordinary care of yourself or another. Saw something inappropriate happening and did what needed to be done. Helped out someone else. It's up to you; just go through your memory and then describe what happened, using as many details as possible. At the conclusion of your story, please describe the strengths, skills and/or characteristics that you demonstrated.

5. Have you ever done something that you were initially afraid of doing? If so, please tell a story about it. Why were you afraid? What allowed you to successfully face your fear? What was that experience like? How did you feel afterwards? What did you learn about yourself?

Mental Illness / Substance Abuse

"A fundamental truth of psychology, from which our ego repeatedly flees, is that it is most commonly through suffering that we are stretched enough to grow spiritually."

James Hollis

Trauma often robs people of a sense that an experience has not just a beginning but an ending, too. Some part of us remains frozen in a destructive experience that is ceaseless reenacted, never coming to a conclusion...One of the benefits of getting unfrozen (in our feelings, actions, plans, responses to people) is how it allows us to get on with our lives – to live as big a life as we would like.

Becky Thompson

We cannot change anything until we accept it. Condemnation does not liberate, it oppresses.

Carl Jung

Change can occur when [a person] abandons, at least for the moment, what he would like to become and attempts to be what he is. The premise is that one must stand in one place in order to have firm footing to move and that it is difficult or impossible to move without that footing.

Arnold Beisser

We may not be able to choose our wounds in life, but we do have the power to choose what those wounds are going to mean.

Jan Goldstein

"...in the midst of these psychological dislocations, we frequently consider ourselves victimized, and cannot imagine that there could be some enlarging purpose arising from our suffering. Often, much later, we are able to recognize that something was moving us purposefully, initiating a new phase of our journey, though it certainly didn't feel like it at the time. We may grudgingly admit that even the suffering enlarged us, and made us more richly human."

James Hollis

Now it is time to explore in more detail your relationship with mental illness and/or substance abuse.

My mental health issue or diagnosis is:

When did your mental health issue first make its presence known in your life? What happened? How did it make you feel? How did your family respond?

What have you been told by others (doctors, family members, friends, the media) regarding your diagnosis or mental health issue?

Please make a list of ten events that stick in your memory that are related to your mental health and/or substance abuse issues.

***

- What my diagnosis or mental health issue says about me:
- How it makes me feel:
- What I believe about it:
- What I have learned from it:
- What I could still learn from it:

***

What or whom have I lost in my life, due to my mental health and/or substance abuse?

How might I grieve and/or honor each of those losses?

What or who in my life has become more important as a result of my mental health issue(s)?

***

Is there another way to view my mental health issue? Could it mean something other than what I currently think it means?

***

Considering the role mental illness or substance abuse in your life, how might you fill in the following:

- I have survived _____ because of my _____
- It was by encountering _____ that I truly understood _____
- After my experience with _____, I learned _____

***

The Hero's Journey provides a framework which you can use to view your life and its challenges in a meaningful way. It allows you to see that throughout history, people have suffered painful events and losses. Yet, according to the Hero's Journey perspective, a crisis may also be an opportunity for growth.

In terms of dealing with your own mental health issues, where are you on the hero's journey framework? Have you already completed one or more journeys? Or are you in the midst of one? In writing, please describe what occurred, using the following template:

- **The Ordinary World:** What was going on in your life **before** you were faced with something "out of the ordinary"?
- **Call to adventure:** What happened that forced you to reconsider how your life had been going? How did the challenge or obstacle arise?
- **Accepting the call:** What allowed you to make the decision to begin moving in a new direction with your life? Why did you decide to move forward and address the challenge instead of ignoring it?
- **Crossing the threshold:** What were some of the first things you did once you committed yourself to facing your challenge?
- **Meeting the mentors:** Who were some people (or animals) you met that helped you? What did they do for you?

- **Facing the ordeal:** What was the toughest thing about overcoming your challenge? How did you successfully handle it?
- **The hero is transformed and receives a reward:** How did you personally change afterward? How did your life change? What did you know after overcoming your challenge that you had not known before?
- **Hero returns home:** What happened next? How did the "new you" impact the other people in your life?

What if you haven't yet started your Hero's Journey? If that is the case, I would like you to imagine that your mental health issue or substance usage is "the call." Using your imagination, can you create a story in which you move through each of the stages successfully? How would that story successfully play out?

Looking towards the future

Our lives are not fixed in stone; instead the paths we take are shaped by story. Thus, how we understand ourselves makes all the difference. If we tell ourselves stories that emphasize our weaknesses, then we become weaker. If those stories focus on our strengths, we tap into a well-spring of personal power. Of course, this is not to suggest that positive narratives eliminate the suffering in our lives. Rather, they allow us to build the resilience and perspective necessary to experience, in meaningful ways, both the joys and sorrows of life.

So think about your current story. Are you reluctant to begin changing it because it might affect another person's story? Who benefits from your current story? What are the costs and benefits if you change? What are the costs and benefits if you don't change? Which payoff is larger?

On a scale from 1 to 10, how committed are you to exploring a new, more empowering narrative for yourself? If the number you chose is less than 10, what would it take to bump that number up just one place?

Please fill in this sentence as many times as you need, using nouns, adjectives and verbs:

- In the future, I would like to be living a life in which I am ---

Based on what you now know about yourself and your story, what would you prefer the main theme of your life to be?

As you think about your future...

What changes do you desire? What different themes would you like to incorporate into your life?

How would you like the roles that you currently play in your life to change?

How would you like your relationship with fear to change?

How would you like to change the relationship you have with the expectations of others?

How will your past story influence your new story?

What will you be doing to empower yourself?

What will your relationship be with spirituality? How will you be connecting with a Higher Power (however you might define that)?

What will you be doing to create happiness / peace / fulfillment?

What will be making your life meaningful?

What patterns would you like to see occurring in your new story?

What adjectives could you use to describe yourself/your life in your new story?

What will be working well for you in your new story? What will you be doing so that those things are working well?

What has worked well for you in the past? How will you continue to incorporate it into your new story? What hasn't worked well for you in the past? How will you avoid repeating those patterns?

In order to create a new story that is empowering for you:

What obstacles will you face? How will you successfully overcome them?

What must you release?

What must you learn?

What skills must you develop?

What will you do to get through difficult times?

Whom must you forgive? What will doing so do for you?

What compromises will you be willing to make?

What commitments will you need to make? With whom? Why will those commitments be important?

***

What disappointments or hurts from the past do you still have strong feelings about?

What is the advantage to holding on to resentment, anger, disappointment and/or regret? What is the disadvantage?

***

Do you have clarity about your dreams and goals? Your heart's desire? If not, what will allow you to gain clarity? What do you need to do?

***

Return to the list of personal values you created earlier. Are there any you need to remove? Add? Rank them in order from most to least important, knowing that you can change the order if you need to in the future.

- Are these values are aligned with the goals you would like to achieve?
- Are these values are aligned with the type of person you would like to become?
- Are these values are aligned with your life's purpose?
- Are these values are compatible with your relationship with your partner?
- Are these values are compatible with other important areas of your life?
- What has to happen for you to live these values on a daily basis?
- How could you begin this process starting today?

***

Now it is time to think about the beliefs that you would you like to have guide your life. These are the beliefs that will empower you and make you feel good about yourself. At the same time, consider those beliefs that have caused you distress or have limited your choices. Are you willing to give yourself permission to release them?

Please make a list using the heading, **I believe that:**

***

"**Personal rules**" are specific non-negotiable commitments you make to yourself and/or others that will allow you to have a meaningful and fulfilling life. These principles can positively influence your how you think and feel because they provide healthy structure and boundaries.

Here are some examples:

- I eat what I want - in moderation
- I avoid sodas
- Breakfast is my biggest meal
- I don't gossip about others
- I drink 8 glasses of water every day
- I go to bed at 9pm at least one time per week
- No matter what time I go to bed, I wake up at 6am every day

- I do not eat after 7pm
- I say "I love you" to my partner at least once a day
- I spend quality time with my child each day
- I give thanks at every meal
- I do some form of exercise every day
- Each night before bed I meditate for five minutes
- I do not check email for at least an hour after I wake up
- No television or computer before bed
- I do not smoke in the car
- I do not eat in front of the TV
- Every other day I write in my gratitude journal
- Every day I spend some time outside in nature
- I pay my bills as soon as I receive them

What are your personal rules? Make a list.

"**Rules for life**" are overarching beliefs which, if you follow them consistently, can also lead to a higher quality of life. They are more general in nature than personal rules and, of course, will be different for each one of us. Think of them as advice you'd give your younger self about how to succeed in life, be happier, and avoid regrets. Here are some examples:

- Always have a pet
- It's OK to accept help
- Be here now
- Treat people right
- Question everything
- Relax

- Listen to music
- Slow down and appreciate the small things
- Aim for excellence
- Keep promises
- Just do it
- Try anything once
- Always be learning something new
- Lead a balanced life
- Know when to quit
- Never give up
- Practice gratitude
- Say 'Please' and 'Thank you'
- Don't hold grudges
- Take responsibility
- It's OK to be vulnerable
- Never assume
- Don't overthink it
- Focus on experiences not possessions
- Think before you speak

What are your own rules for life?

***

You are on your death bed, looking back on your life. In the end, what was it that made your life worth living?

***

What ritual or ceremony can you use to represent closure of your old story and welcome your new story?

Can you create something artistically (a painting, sculpture, collage) to represent an aspect of your old story? What might you do with it when you're done that would feel healing?

Can you create something artistically to represent your new narrative or a new theme that you'd like to incorporate into your life? What might you do with it so that it becomes an empowering daily reminder for you?

**

Thinking about the stories we tell about ourselves can make an enormous difference in the ways we live our lives. Drawing on the field of narrative therapy and the Hero's Journey, my goal in this book has been to give you some ideas to help you help your clients rewrite and retell their own stories.

I believe it is so important for our clients, who are dealing with different degrees of mental illness and substance abuse, to experience the power of personal responsibility and resourcefulness. It is vital for them to understand their gifts and unique abilities, as well as discover that sometimes their greatest weakness can also be their greatest strength. Indeed, an important lesson to learn is that the tragedies we experience in life also contain the seeds of positive change.

By understanding the framework of the Hero's Journey – a timeless aspect of what it means to be human – our clients can begin to recognize that obstacles and challenges are an integral part of the recovery process, and see set-backs as opportunities for personal growth and self-development. After all, what the Hero's Journey teaches us is that life is cyclical, with a continual series of smaller journeys made up of their own beginnings, middles and ends. And each of those journeys needs to be recognized and honored (and even celebrated).

As clinicians, we have an important role in assisting our clients in manifesting their full potential. In fact, our presence is integral because we serve as an important witness to the process of re-authoring. After all, for our clients the prospect of answering "the call" is scary, and so it is imperative that they have support and validation.

It is also vital to communicate our belief to the client that they are a worthy human being who has the capacity to live through a crisis and grow from the experience. We can often spot strengths and resources in the client's life that the client may have overlooked. We can also ensure that the client figures out meaningful ways to grieve their losses and celebrate their achievements.

By sharing the Hero's Journey framework with our clients, we can show them that each one of us are the experts of our own experiences and that the road to a fulfilling, meaningful life will be different for every person.

But perhaps, when all is said and done, the most liberating and radical aspect of the Hero's Journey that we can share with our clients is that it views distress as a beginning, not an ending. It demonstrates that a mental health disorder does not have to constrain their lives. Quite the opposite: What appears to be an ending is actually a beginning – an invitation to the road to recovery.

Appendix:
Creating a Manifesto

A manifesto is a declaration of your principles. It summarizes who you are, what you do and why you do it. It's your point of view.

A manifesto incorporates your strengths, values, and passions, as well as your goals and aims in life. As both a call to action and mission statement, it is designed to be shared with others as a public proclamation. By formally stating the beliefs and intentions that guide your life, you are reminding others as well as yourself why you are here and why you matter.

Manifestos come in all shapes and sizes. Some are short written statements (The Declaration of Independence) while others are books (The Communist Manifesto) or even speeches (I have a Dream). Others are lists or a series of slogans. Some manifestos are creatively rendered, incorporating different sized fonts or colorful artwork. If you simply google "manifestos images" you will be presented with a wide array of examples to use as models and inspiration!

The topic of a manifesto is up to you and there are no rules. At its simplest it states what is important to you. It could reflect your philosophy of life in general or describe your place in the world.

Your manifesto could focus on a particular area of your life that you feel strongly about (such as family, career, faith, mental health recovery). Or it might specifically highlight one or more of the following: Values / Goals / Principles / Beliefs / Personal Policies / Rules for Living / The Purpose of Life .

Creating a manifesto gives you the opportunity to become clear about who you are and what you stand for. As a source of inspiration that you can see or read on a daily basis, having a manifesto present in your life will make it easier to pull through tough times.

Examples of Manifestos

Apple

1. We believe that we're on the face of the earth to make great products.

2. We're constantly focusing on innovating.

3. We believe in the simple, not the complex.

4. We believe we need to own and control the primary technologies behind the products that we make and participate only in markets where we can make a significant contribution.

5. We believe in saying no to thousands of projects so that we can focus on the few that are meaningful to us.

6. We believe in deep collaboration and cross pollination in order to innovate in a way others cannot.

7. We don't settle for anything other than excellence in any group in the company.

8. We have the self-honesty to admit when we're wrong and the courage to change.

The Slow Manifesto (Christopher Richards)

There are those who urge us to speed. We resist! We shall not flag or fail. We shall slow down in the office, and on the roads. We shall slow down with growing confidence when all those around us are in a shrill state of hyperactivity (signifying nothing). We shall defend our state of calm, whatever the cost may be. We shall slow down in the fields and in the streets, we shall slow down in the hills, we shall never surrender! If you can slow down when all around you are speeding up, then you're one of us. Be proud that you are one of us and not one of them. For they are fast, and we are slow. If a thing is *worth doing, it is* worth doing slowly. Some are born to slowness—others have it thrust upon them. And still others know that lying in bed with a morning cup of tea is the supreme state for mankind.

Austin Kleon

1. Steal like an artist.
2. Don't wait until you know who you are to get started.
3. Write the book you want to read.
4. Use your hands.
5. Side projects and hobbies are important.
6. The secret: do good work and share it with people.
7. Geography is no longer our master.
8. Be nice. (The world is a small town.)
9. Be boring. (It's the only way to get work done.)
10. Creativity is subtraction.

The Linchpin Manifesto (Seth Godin)

Yes. Now. I am an artist. • I take initiative • I do the work, not the job. • Without critics, there is no art. • I am a Linchpin. I am not easily replaced. • If it's never been done before, even better. • The work is personal, too important to phone in. • The lizard brain is powerless in the face of art. • I make it happen. Every day. • Every interaction is an opportunity to make a connection. • The past is gone. It has no power. The future depends on choices I make now. • I own the means of production—the system isn't as important as my contribution to it. • I see the essential truth unclouded by worldview, and that truth drives my decisions. • I lean into the work, not away from it. Trivial work doesn't require leaning. • Busywork is too easy. Rule-breaking works better and is worth the effort. • Energy is contagious. The more I put in, the more the world gives back. • It doesn't matter if I'm always right. It matters that I'm always moving. • I raise the bar. I know yesterday's innovation is today's standard. • I will not be brainwashed into believing in the status quo. • Artists don't care about credit. We care about change. • There is no resistance if I don't allow it to defeat me. • I embrace a lack of structure to find a new path. • I am surprising. (And often surprised). • I donate energy and risk to the cause. • I turn charisma into leadership. • The work matters. • Go. Make something happen.

Gretchen Rubin's Happiness Manifesto

- To be happy, you need to consider feeling good, feeling bad, and feeling right, and an atmosphere of growth.
- One of the best ways to make *yourself* happy is to make *other people* happy; one of the best ways to make *other people* happy is to be happy *yourself*.
- The days are long, but the years are short.
- You're not happy unless you think you're happy.
- Your body matters.
- Happiness is other people.
- Think about yourself so you can forget yourself.
- "It is easy to be heavy: hard to be light." — G. K. Chesterton
- What's fun for other people may not be fun for you, and vice versa.
- Best is good, better is best.
- Outer order contributes to inner calm.
- Happiness comes not from having more, not from having less, but from wanting what you have.
- You can choose what you do, but you can't choose what you *like* to do.
- You manage what you measure.
- "There is no duty we so much underrate as the duty of being happy." — Robert Louis Stevenson

The Daily Decalogue of Pope John XXIII

1. Only for today, I will seek to live the livelong day positively without wishing to solve the problems of my life all at once.

2. Only for today, I will take the greatest care of my appearance: I will dress modestly; I will not raise my voice; I will be courteous in my behavior; I will not criticize anyone; I will not claim to improve or to discipline anyone except myself.

3. Only for today, I will be happy in the certainty that I was created to be happy, not only in the other world but also in this one.

4. Only for today, I will adapt to circumstances, without requiring all circumstances to be adapted to my own wishes.

5. Only for today, I will devote 10 minutes of my time to some good reading, remembering that just as food is necessary to the life of the body, so good reading is necessary to the life of the soul.

6. Only for today, I will do one good deed and not tell anyone about it.

7. Only for today, I will do at least one thing I do not like doing; and if my feelings are hurt, I will make sure that no one notices.

8. Only for today, I will make a plan for myself: I may not follow it to the letter, but I will make it. And I will be on guard against two evils: hastiness and indecision.

9. Only for today, I will firmly believe, despite appearances, that the good Providence of God cares for me as no one else who exists in this world.

10. Only for today, I will have no fears. In particular, I will not be afraid to enjoy what is beautiful and to believe in goodness. Indeed, for 12 hours I can certainly do what might cause me consternation were I to believe I had to do it all my life.

JetSetCitizen Manifesto (John Bardos)

Simplify: Consume less. Live more.

Live Healthy: Eat right, exercise and don't do stupid things. Without health, you have nothing.

Pursue Excellence: Improve yourself a little every day. You are what you repeatedly do.

Challenge Yourself: Temporary setbacks now, are much better than lifelong regrets.

Cultivate Relationships: People are everything. Give more than you take and respect differences.

Experience the World: Life is short. There is a big world out there to explore.

Contribute: Billions of people still live on less than $2 per day. You are one of the lucky ones, so share that good fortune.

My Manifesto (Shawn Phelps)

I want to be part of a revolution
where we all deeply understand our own unique value;
where we stop looking to others to tell us
who we should be and what we should care about;
where we show up as our whole, authentic selves–
with the courage to share our secret fears and feelings;
where we make a difference just by being
all that we've always been,
because we finally feel our own magnificence,
and "get" that we are the divine, expressed;
and where, above all, we are guided by our True Self,
which wants only to take us on a great adventure
toward our happiest life and highest potential.
Because that's why we came here.
And because that's what we all deserve.
Every. Last. One. Of. Us.
Every. One.
One.

My Symphony (William Henry Channing)

To live content with small means; to seek elegance rather than luxury, and refinement rather than fashion, to be worthy, not respectable, and wealthy, not rich; to study hard, think quietly, talk gently, act frankly, to listen to stars and birds, to babes and sages, with open heart, to bear all cheerfully, to all bravely await occasions, hurry never. In a word, to let the spiritual unbidden and unconscious grow up through the common. This is to be my symphony.

Made in the USA
Monee, IL
16 April 2023

31960196R00059